# Bastards

##                                             &      Bitches

--- And ---

## *LOVE*

                    …one of my favorite

                                          subjects

Sir Finis DeMilo Brewer

Copyright 2015

By: SIR FINIS DeMILO BREWER

Published by:

TOOSWEETPUBLISHING productions

P.O. Box 6512 New Orleans, LA. 70174

ISBN: 978-0-941091-20-6

ALL RIGHTS RESERVED

No part of this book may be reproduced in any form without the written permission of the publisher.

First Printing

PRINTED IN THE UNITED STATES OF AMERICA

This Book is

Dedicated to my three (3)

***BEST (female) FRIENDS***

for more than 40 years

**Drea, Gwen, Val**

who have known me,

my "ups & downs";

trials & tribulations

and my DREAMS

and knows that **SIR**

is not just my name;

it's who I AM

# TABLES OF CONTENTS

1. BASTARDS & BITCHES

2. LOVE…my favorite Subject
   a. March 5, Easter Sunday
   b. My KURSTENS
   c. Miss Sangi / Na-She
   d. Back to Miss Sangi

3. FINAL CHAPTER

# Bastards and Bitches

A few weeks ago after I decided to resurrect my "closet" writing career, and write full-time without a "9to5" (because I could not seem to GET a "9to5"). I began to read again with such fervor, that I lost count of the many books I read in the first week I began to write again. Often time when I read a book, it may make reference to another book. And, if I find the subject or title interesting, I'll make it a candidate to read the book mentioned as well.

In the course of reading one book (I can't remember the title, or author), I ran across a title of a book interestingly called "The Bastard on the Couch". It was a very good read; stories about men and their confessions concerning their feelings about women. And the prelude to this title was another book (I think,…written by the same author, but don't quote me cause I tend to not concentrate on the creator, just the creation), titled "The Bitch in the House;" It too, was interesting but not as much to me as the "guy" book, "The Bastard On the Couch."

 As I read the women's book, I'm disturbed by the content. To me, the book comes across as stories about a bunch of women trying to find themselves, while many don't really know what they want, and most find themselves in the "world of careers," constantly feeling like they have to prove something, and compete with Man.  Some of the women saw men in their lives as if they were a type of dildo, a "tool" that they use, at their leisure and convenience. And when they were done (satisfied), they would just toss "it/them" aside.

When I imagine a female / woman / chick girl in my life, I imagine them as a partner. Someone that shares like interests has like desires, and they're sure about themselves as a young woman, and sure of their "GOD given" beauty. Not needing a man (or anyone) to validate their beauty, their gifts, or their talents. They know who they are; and they are not like putty in the hands of a Potter, being shaped by the distorted and the sick opinions, of this very "sick" world. Where "anything goes" now, and no one worries about the consequences.

If a female know who they are, know their destiny, and if GOD has brought my life together with their life, there is nothing we won't be able to accomplish…together. That's how I picture the "lady" person in my life, and that's what I prefer. And I say "lady person" intently because I'm not interested in any female that thinks she is just as much "man" as I am. When she drinks her tea, her pinky is noticeable; when she sits in a chair her legs are not as wide as the Panama canal; and when she is making love to me, it is me she is thinking about, and not some "hunk" she saw on some magazine cover, or wanna be rapper she saw in a video. I am her "hunk," and she is my lady like queen. And she doesn't need a nightstand full of dildos; different sizes & different colors like some confused, "don't know what she wants" BITCH in heat. And in this day and age, so many have degraded down to this shocking & disappointing level.

 I know I used to put the female (in general) on a pedestal, and I did it because I always saw them from GOD's perspective. Next to Christ as far as I was concern, they were the greatest gift GOD gave to man. And I still feel, and believe that. But…women today seem to be confused, and so unsatisfied. And the degree in which they have devalued themselves by thinking it's cute to sleep with lots of guys, cute to be a "project queen," or welfare & Section 8 recipient baffles me. Or to think it's cute to have 3,4,5 (or more) babies with different daddies, is mind blowin, and defies everything GOD wants for womankind.

I'm sure He had much better plans for the "daughters of Eve" of this generation; but just like in the Garden of Eden, give them too much "rope" (or room), and she's gonna hang herself. We know it happen then, and we see it still happening now. And I know many might think that I'm sounding a bit chauvinistic, "but I ain't got nuthin but Love for ya baby!...nuthin but LOVE for ya!"

When a woman began to think she is as much "man" as man is, she is in trouble. Look at lesbianism for instance; it's a demonic spirit that lies to the female and tells her she is man too. She can "satisfy" a women better than a man can…and it's all just a "pack of Lies" to deceive the women.

Satan hasn't changed; he is still up to his "old tricks" to kill, steal, and destroy. And why so many are shock when things don't work out when they listen to satan, just amazes me. It's like jumping in a body of water, and wondering why you are wet…DA DUH!

…"YOU JUMPED IN THE DAM WATER!"

I've been divorced twice; and I loved both of my wives faithfully. One more than the other because, one I knew I was divinely chosen to be with, and the other I knew I chose myself. Nevertheless, I did my part as a husband, provided for my children without govt assistance, kept a job, and loved my wives & children unconditionally without a fuss or fight (at least not until they were busted); then there was some fussing.

But looking back, I realized that they both suffered from the same condition (some say it was their youth, I disagreed); they both Lied a lot, Lied to themselves, and always needed to be validated by someone (or something) outside of themselves. And because I chose not to be worldly (friends with the world), and I chose to be a

"Christian" instead, I lost them both to the world, and things of the world. Like Sex outside of marriage, and more sex, drugs, drinking, and partying. They no longer wanted the "Christian life" of living "right"; they found it to be boring. But it was ok if they were sick, or someone in their family was sick, or had a need. Then it was,

"Oh babe, can you pray for my brother,"

"Or, lets pray and ask GOD to give us a new car."

…and the request went on and on.

But when satan came a knocking, they fell "hook, line, and sinker" with both legs "wide" open…and that to me was the most hurting part. Because I knew, they were better than that; I know a "good thing" when I see it, and I know what I saw in both of them in the beginning. And the "dog" they both chose were just that…"dogs;" and both of them had all the characteristics of a "dog." Humps anything that lets it, and don't love nobody; not even themselves. If even the Bible says,

"Beware of dogs"

I think it's a legitimate warning, and deserves taking heed to.

Eventually, I recovered from the hurt & pain of the betrayal, but I know it changed me forever. I don't see women the same, and because of the "pollution" called music that is being pumped in the ears of so many young girls coming up today, their condition is even worse than the young girls that was coming up during my time, or thereafter. They have no sense of respect for themselves or their bodies, no respect for their parents, engaging in bisexual & lesbianism is rampant amongst some as young as 12 years old, and the value of virginity competing with promiscuity, is like an old rusty penny trying to compete with a $100 dollar bill…no chance!

Often I thought about what it would take to forgive my wife and take her back, being that we have 3 lovely daughters together. But I know that because of her way of thinking (and her stupid-ass "no husband" friends filling up her head with continual stupidity) she would think that going back to her husband would be a step back. But because of what I've learn, what I know to be truth, and who GOD has made me, I know better. "Dicks" are a dime a dozen, and so are "whores on magic sticks," but you can't buy respect, and having money doesn't make a difference. You're just a "ho" with money; and ya still a "bitch" in the eyes of every dick you sucked.

So, is this type of reputation you want? Is it better than that of a respectable wife?

…I think not!!!

Every wife I married, I married out of respect for them, and out of respect for GOD. And they were well respected while they were married to me. Now if you were to ask them if they prefer the life they have now (and since had), to the respectable life they once had, if they said they prefer the life they have now? I would "smh" and say,

"You are still Lying to yourself…(You dumb-Ass)"

A woman has to know she's loved, she's appreciated, and she is not playing "second fiddle" to anything or anyone in her Man's life. If a woman says these things don't matter to her, again I would say,

"YOU ARE LYING TO YOURSELF."

(Dumb-Ass)

No matter who we are, are where you come from, we are who we are by GOD's design; that's male & female because that's who HE said HE made us to be. Now anything other than that, its man's creation, not GOD's.

Working in the Nursery at the hospital, I've seen babies born with all types of conditions; and dealing with people daily and studying them, I see people develop into all types of personality. And you know what I've concluded?

...GOD cannot take credit for any of it; only man.

We have so many additives in our food today; babies are born with all kinds of conditions & problems. And we grow up still eating foods with many additives, and the problems these additives creates, continues. And people have been feed so many "lies" (and has believed them) throughout the years, that it has created a very twisted generation with some very twisted ideas about GOD & life. This has created problems. So when it's all said & done, GOD is not the author of all this "confusion" on the earth and in the minds of so many people.

…We ARE our problem, and we created them (and are creating more each day); not GOD.

So looking back on this life I've lived, I can honestly say I have been gravely disappointed in some things. But mostly in the lack of Honesty, that we show one another. I have loved many people in my lifetime; romantic & otherwise. I've written many poems & stories about people I've loved. But under no circumstance has any person (romantic or otherwise) has ever been obligated to LOVE me back. LOVE should always be given in all sincerity, and with "no strings" attached. And if, and when you give LOVE, please don't confuse it with LUST, or SEX. These are two "destructive forces" that are not in the same league with LOVE.

…Never have been, and NEVER will be.

And to those who think SEX and LOVE is the same, let me explain;…THEY ARE NOT!!! .

If you LOVE someone, and they LOVE you the same, genuinely & sincerely with no legal or moral obligations to another, and that LOVE does not defy "natural law" concerning SEX, then the experience that your "Body & Soul" share is LOVE, not sex.

Because SEX, just like its twin (LUST), comes out of selfish desires. Selfish desires that don't care who gets hurt by their selfish activities, or desires. If it breaks up a family, so what; if it devastates a spouse, who cares!...what I want is all that matters!

"Does any of this sound familiar?"

"Have you ever found yourself "wearing these shoes?"

...I'm sure many of you have, if LIFE is all about what you want.

I have Live long enough to know…

"Mama ain't raised no fool; and GOD is not Man, that HE should LIE…;"

And no matter how much time passes in life, Man & Woman was made for each other. And the one gender will never do better, without the other."

That doesn't mean that every Man & Woman was meant to be…together. GOD has always had a divine purpose and plan for each Man & each Woman. Unfortunately, many just don't want to hear GOD's plan, for their life. Everybody wants to do their "own thing," make their own money, and create and serve their own gods.

Well every civilization that thought like this, no longer exist. We are a "creation" created by GOD, and if anyone has the "key" to our lives (or the answers) HE does.

So whether you are the "BITCH IN THE HOUSE" or "THE BASTARD ON THE COUCH," neither condition is the fault of GOD. But more than likely result of your own selfish desire to "do your own thing"; be your own man, or be your own woman.

If a 2 year old child can look up at its parents and say,

"I don't care what you say; I'm going to do whatever I want to, when I want to, and how I want to!"

And you can see how foolish and "dangerously ignorant" that is, than the selfish & foolish generation of today is just like that 2 year old when it comes to not listening to GOD.

I thank GOD that I'm neither a "Bastard or a Bitch"; I'm a grateful, and blessed young man, father & grand-Papi of a proud and beautiful brood. Loved dearly by both my parents, all my family and friends, with no qualms or reservations about showing love to my fellow man (especially strangers)…because sometimes we "entertain Angels unawares.." I'm also blessed with a compassionate enough heart to admit and say "I'm sorry" when

I'm wrong, or extend a heart of forgives when I've been wronged. Why am I like this?

…Because JESUS died on the Cross for all of our wrong doings, and when I stand before GOD, I won't have a case to rail against

No man (or wife), or be able to cry,

"Oh Lord, woe is me; I can't believe they done me like that"

…because of "HIS Blood" that is on this Cross.

For the Bible says,

"…unless there is a shedding of blood, there is no remission for sins.."

Now some of you may not even believe in the Bible; and that's your "free-will" choice, like everything else in life. But we all got to believe in something, or somebody; and especially ourselves.

So rather than being a "Bastard or a Bitch," or seeing yourself as such due to low self esteem, or distorted & false messages from external sources outside of our own selves, let us all try and strive to be "Children of GOD," or at least see ourselves as such. For the benefits of doing so, far outweigh the end results of us being "Bitches, or Bastards."

The End…for now.

'THE Game called… I LOVE YOU'

This is the I LOVE YOU game
It lasted till you were 21;
Then you met a stranger on face book
And now you have a son

When you said I love you
I guess it was just words
Because the feeling didn't stay long
It flew away like a bird

People make promises
And commitments everyday

They think GOD is deaf

And can't hear what they say

But he hears when you say I LOVE YOU

And he hears all the cuss words to;

And to those who didn't grow up in church

He also sees the things you do


And one day when you are old

If you live long enough to get there;

You will be judged by your words

And for the times you didn't care…


…A thing about GOD

Or, what HE said not to do;

When he hands down the punishment

It will fall on YOU

Not on satan the devil
Because he made you do it;
Not on your maw or paw
Even though they both knew it

…That you had a few problems
With commitments, Lying, & Sex;
No, GOD won't blame them
For Your husband now being your Ex

HE will say, "Child of mine"
I had a better plan for your life;
Instead of being a whore to the world

I made plans for you to be a good man's wife

But I gave you "freewill" when I created you

And reminded you that your soul was not for sale;

But you sold it to satan anyway

And now you're heading towards HELL

Remember this was not my choice for you

The path I chose was custom made;

A husband, children, and a great LIFE

But you didn't listen to a Word I said

Satan got your attention

Like he did your "Mother Eve" in the Garden;

And generation after generation is still thinking

The crap from him is a bargain

In exchange for "pseudo-freedom"

He has given much sickness & all types of disease;

Even fooled many with a gay lifestyle that is not ok

Just doing whatever they please

No thought of tomorrow

No thought of the consequences;

Living in Sin saying they are Christians

While they straddle all kinds of "fences"

But GOD is not fooled

HE sees all that we do;

I just hope you get it together one day

…Before HE allow satan to come and get YOU.

SIR D. BREWER
11-25-2013 / 4 a.m.
(Couldn't sleep one night a few days ago; this is what came out of that sleepless night)

The history of this next Poem, was written for a friend of mine that I later learned was too nice and beautiful to be doing what she was doing.

When it was written, I know the Holy Spirit was leading me to write, but at the time I didn't know why. The person in question, because they were young I thought they were still a virgin. But looking at her lifestyle from a distance, I learned otherwise. So it was written for her, and believe it or not, I was lead by the Holy Spirit to do so.

 I guess it was a self-esteem issue, because there was no other way in which I could explain the behavior of such a young person.

I don't know what makes a young girl give herself to boys or men, and some that are complete stranger, but it has to be a self esteem issue.

I thank GOD that I've never needed affirmation from anyone. I always have known who I am. Some have called me arrogant, thinking I'm better than others, but that is so far from the truth. My confidence rests in the CHRIST that I know & serve. Even as a kid, I was comfortable with me, and didn't need anyone's accolades. I have written many pieces about the quality I see in the female, and at some point I realize I had put them all on pedestals. And of course, over time I began to see them in a different light. No one is the same, so we can't expect people to all act & be the same.

But, whether they all are different, it doesn't explain this current trend amongst the 18 & up (sometimes younger) to aspire to be "twerking queens," "thug trophy," "stripper pole champions " and "G-string video vixens". What happen to the "girl next door" or the ones to proudly take home to Mom? Do they even exist anymore? …I wonder.

And when it comes to the ones with children, them having three & four different Daddies (baby donors is more like it) is crazy to me. I just have always believed that GOD had a much better plan. And if we would just stick to it, Life is guaranteed to be better.

I guess I sound like I'm preaching, but that's what I was called to do. And thank GOD, I was not like some who preach and say, "do as I say & not as I do." I have always respected the youthfulness & virginity of a young girl. Even when I was in my teens as well. Opportunity presented itself often, and I admit I would have love to take certain ones up on that offer, but I couldn't. If their mother trusted me, I valued that. I wasn't going to lose their trust, by "spoiling their daughter" as my older brother would say.

But it never was Sex for me; it was always about LOVE. And I guess that's what made me different from my generation. Yea I was accused of being "funny" as it was called back then. Because I was always surrounded by "girls"; and they were sometimes always offering themselves. And in all my many years here on earth and all the chances I had to be "naughty" there have been only three times in my life that I really, really, wanted to accommodate them. Out of the three, one I married, and the other two their mother trusted me; and I couldn't let them down. I loved them both, and would have given them the world. I won't reveal their but names, but just realized I wrote a piece about all three (3) of them. And the titles of each piece I wrote, ends with "Eyes"…Wow!

Well the Bible says, the "Eyes are the windows to our souls"; so it must be something to my being taken smitten by their eyes before I was captivated by their bodies…umm…very interesting. I guess I am a 4EVER Romantic.

To ..ALL the **PYT's** and… *my friend*

## *"DON'T GIVE YOUR BEAUTY AWAY"*

Don't Give Your Beauty Away Pretty One

It will keep you from the Fires of Hell

For the Body is the Temple of the HOLY Spirit

And it lets the Devil know it's not for sale

I look at you and I cringe

Because I see such a familiar face

You remind me and look, like someone very dear to me

Who is no longer in a Right, or Good place

She gave her Beauty away one day

And allow it to be treated like Trash

She thought it was cool to Lie with "dogs"

Who hated GOD and loved drugs & cash


They say most young Girls are foolish

Easily giving their hearts & souls to "Boys"

Losing their virginity and blessings from GOD

To foolish "dudes" still playing with toys


So many are taught & believe the Lie

That they are too young for a Husband & Marriage

Yet it's ok to live like a whorish Jezebel

Becoming a welfare recipient with a Baby carriage

Fun ain't fun if it cost YOU

Time, Money, or your Life

So please stop giving your Beauty away

It's better to be a beautiful wife

The Blessings you get is beyond measure

The Benefits beats the immoral "trash"

Hang on to the Beauty GOD has given you

And don't ever trade it for cash

To me, every "Eve" is beautiful and a gift
                                      from GOD

And more valuable than precious Jewels
                                      & pure Gold

But every Young Girl must know and believe this in their own heart

   …that True Love last,

and lustful Sex gets old


So hang on to your Goodness, Pretty One…

Don't give your Beauty away, I pray

It's too precious, and too priceless to lose

And Sex without marriage… is just not ok


Plus, your heart is too precious & fragile

And your Soul is worth even more

And Your Body should never be abused

Because that's not what it was meant for

YES, society says "Go ahead, do your thang!'

Do what makes you feel good, and weak

But that's how we got AIDs, Herpes, and other diseases

Because what we Sow, we shall also Reap

It will be worth the wait… I promise

Because GOD's favor is worth the sacrifice

The things GOD has for those who wait

Will guarantee them a better Life

GOD has so much HE wants to Give US

HE says it in the written WORD

Eyes have not seen, or entered in the Heart

And Ears have not even heard

If we Love GOD we will do Our Best

To Honor GOD, and do what's Right

No matter what the World do, or say is cool

We will walk like the "Children of the Light"

I'm gonna end this Literary Piece now

I hope you listened closely, and learned

                          a thang or two

Save Your Body & Beauty… for ONE who Loves GOD

And the ONE GOD chose, and picked for YOU

      SIR FINIS DeMilo BREWER    4/23/13 12:53am

Looking back, I realized that I've been in love with the "Daughters of EVE" all my life. Even in elementary, I was smitten by their incredible artistic Beauty of the female, No matter the age, no matter the race or culture; they are Beautiful. Next to Christ, the female is the Greatest Gift GOD has given to Man. And satan knows this; that's why he attacks their minds with low-self esteem issues, and self- worth. He can't take their value or beauty away, but he'll fool them into destroying themselves by over-eating, under eating, allowing men to abuse them, jumping on crazy "band-wagons" like feminist moments, girl power this & gay that as if Man is their enemy. But man is there other half. What good is anything if it's only half. So no matter who you are, what you grow up to be, or how much money you have made in this life, the positions you hold in this life…you are still a half. And the same thing applies to the Man. When I think of my Daughters when they were little, and my Grand-daughters that still are little, they bring me a joy that often leave me speechless because I LOVE them so. And I know how much they mean to GOD… each and every last one of them. But I have never had any desire for any of them to grow up and be "somebody" like the world teaches them (doctors, lawyers, etc). They are already SOMEBODY to me, and definitely to GOD. There role in Life is to be Happy and fulfilled whatever destiny GOD has ordained for them…be it Doctor, Lawyer, Teacher, etc. And I know it includes a husband in their life, so that they may also be a Mother. Which is the Greatest role on earth, because it is the only role in life, that brings LIFE, and changes the whole UNIVERSE.

I'm so very proud of the :Daughters of Eve" that GOD has blessed me with. They KNOW Daddy/Papi Loves them, and they mean the world to me. And all I require of them is to Be good to themselves, and LOVE GOD.

And how do we love GOD?...by keeping HIS Commandments.

And this is the same thing that our Heavenly Father has required of all his "Daughters"…be good to yourselves, and LOVE Him. But you can't LOVE HIM if you don't KNOW him…and satan knows this. And this is why he has caused ALL the "confusion" that he has in the world.

Growing up, I really love Nature; all the Beauty that it possess. And I love photographing this awesome Beauty and capturing that moment and taking it with me. Like a majestic mountain; a beautiful 100 year old Oak tree; a gorgeous Sunset; and an ocean or lake view is breath-taking. But the image of a beautiful young female is a true Artist "eye candy". Not to Lust after, but just to be admired at GOD's wonderful creation. Michelangelo knew it, David Hamilton knew it, and so did the "fallen angels". Who was so smitten by their form and image, that they fell from Heaven. And that tells you the power of the young women.

But it was never a power to be abused, miss used, or to be confused. It was a power to be loved & shared with one man, one at a time, as his husband. And when a Man loves you…there is nothing that GOD will withhold from this man, to give to you. But that Man, must be the Man that HE has given to you. Not one you have picked yourself. For your Father in Heaven knows what is best for you, more than you do.

### "When I was Three (3)"

*I once met a girl*

*When I three (3);*

*She was so Pretty,*

*And very good to me*

*And when I made five (5)*

*She punched me in the Eye*

*Now I'm in Love,*

*And too blind to see*

SIR 10/6/2014 11:44p.m.

"Beauty & Innocence"

Growing up in the 70's, 80's, and 90's, I had many beautiful girls to write about. I even have copies of pieces I've written when I was as young as 12 or 13 yrs old. All of them forever immortalize in print as that beautiful "daughter of Eve" and creation of GOD, that stirred my heart. Later when I was older, a few more names were added to the list.

Brown Eyes; Tiffani; a "mystery one" whom I would never divulge their name; and a few strangers whom I never knew their names.

Great qualities and attributes, with a hint of innocence still lingering. Showcasing that pure heart & genuine kindness that hasn't been corrupted by a wicked & evil world.

But nowadays I don't get much to write about when it comes to the "daughters of Eve". I have been married twice, and greatly disappointed twice because they both, did not know their worth, or saw what I saw in them. Now as a single man again, I don't write as much about the "daughters of Eve" because the world has changed. And so have the "daughters". They are more like the daughters of jezebel, than the daughters of Eve. Females have changed so tremendously, till I can go the whole day, and see 100's of them in a day, all shapes, ages, and shades. Long hair, short hair, no hair; and out of that bunch, if I notice one, it's been a good day for me as an Artist & Writer. So many don't have their own hair, own nails, own breast, own butt, own mind, or own man. And many have turned to their own gender…what a travesty we are living in.

I'm a natural Artist that sees beauty in ways that many may miss. The gift of being able to discern, the "good from the evil"; the "Light from the darkness"; and the Lady from the "Jezebel" is a gift I value.

 I've noticed growing up, that most of us all are born with the "light & goodness" in us. But this Evil & Wicked World has driven it out of us by the time we become adults.

The Bible says "suffer the little children, and forbid them not; for such is the kingdom of Heaven. Which means you have to have the pure & unselfish heart of a child… to LOVE the right way; LIVE the right way; and to get to Heaven.

" This journey we all have been enlisted to take here on earth, is a very short journey compare to the time we'll spent in the hereafter. But how you spend your time here on earth, greatly determines where you will spend the hereafter. Now some say there is no such place; that after you are dead, you are done. In my journey here, I've come to know… better than that.

# For the One that Changed

It's ok if we changed

As long as we change for the better,

And since today was your birthday

I thought I would write you this letter;

Six years ago yesterday

You gave me our first daughter,

But somehow things have changed

And you now have a child with a different father

But all is forgiven

At least on my part,

GOD is still pretty good to me

In spite of you breaking four (4) Hearts

The Hearts of our three (3) children
And the Heart of their Father,
But Life isn't over
When you have taste the "Living Waters"

I forgave years ago
Even before the change occurred,
Now I hope you forgive yourself
And get back in GOD's Word

Life goes On, as I end this poem,
Even though so much has changed;
You never changed from Smith

And I felt it was bullshit

Only on paper was Brewer your last name

Playing this "ILUVU" game


Happy 23th Birthday Ex-friend

October 2012 was the official end

When you gave soul & body to another;

It was such a sad Day

But that's what you wanted…to f-ing play

And lost your role as Best Wife & Mother


Too bad the Love came to an END

GOD gave you the best that HE had;

But HIS Best wasn't good enough for you

Yet why you still cussing & mad

You lie to yourself saying U fine

But I know ya, but U say I don't

If you were then, who U are now

You would have never been something I would want


Perfect LOVE that is lost

Always comes with a cost

And the heart gets dark & sad

Because not one single day was ever bad

… it was a GOOD THANG, what we had


But you chose to believe the LIE

And it brought tears to my eyes,

It was good while it lasted

And the LOVE was fantastic

But it all came to an end

When you chose the thug & the SIN

You were not the person I married

You were always cussin, fussin, & High

And your change tried to destroy me

and the Evil Spirit of LUST,

…was the reason why.

10-16-13/3-23-15

SIR FINIS DeMILO BREWER

My very first "Literary piece" for 2014…

"WHAT SOME COUPLES DO TO LOVE"

As I began to write this piece, I realize this was my very first piece since the New Year began. And of course, it's always something simple that seems to trigger my need to write. This time around, I was on the internet and I had just click on a sight showing Bridal dresses. Some were ugly, and I guess as I thought about the "LOVE part" of weddings…the words just began to flow. Five minutes later, I have another great perspective & "literary piece" about LOVE…

I think it's a shame what some couples do to LOVE. At one time in their lives,

LOVE to them was the greatest thing since fresh air; they couldn't stand to be apart from one another. Then hatred, deceit, and distrust knocks on the door, and they let the "destroyers" in.

*...now they can't stand the sight of one another, or even be in the same room.*

Do they not realize that LOVE and LOYALTY goes hand in hand? And FAITH and TRUST are brother & sister when it comes to Marriage?

When you LOVE someone being loyal to them comes easy; and when you are loyal, hurting them never enters your mind. Nor will you allow anyone else to hurt them.

I'm very grateful to the many that have taught me about LOVE, and how to LOVE. From the complete stranger, to the brief acquaintance; the friend turn lover and Lover turn friend. Both young & older,…and the few precious innocence of some. Overall, I've had some great teachers when it came to LOVE.

But I'm glad that not many know me intimately.

*A wife or two…*

*… a mistake ( I made a few);*

*But if I count it all on one hand,*

*I won't get all the way through.*

I just believe that some things in life should not be shared with the whole world.

One's Body…for instance. Should everyone that have seen you on TV, also should have seen your "gift"? Or imagine,…you walk into a room with over one hundred women in attendance. And every last one of them know how endowed you are; or what your face look like when you reach a climax. Would that be something to be proud of?

Or imagine,…you are a beautiful young lady; you are getting married. Every guy there (10, 20, 30, maybe more) all know "your name" and have heard you call theirs. Is that pretty?

I think not.

The world (or whole school, neighborhood) shouldn't know your flavor; some "sweets" should be shared with just a few, or not shared at all…Just reserve for someone special.

I love the fact that not many "know my name" and never will. I have always reserved that position for very special people in my life.

LOVE is one of those "beautiful things" in life that all should know, and experience at least once in their life. Thankfully, I had the pleasure of being in love all my life, and all the time. Being in love with a pretty face; and sweet voice; a walk on the beach; a sunset; a beautiful body; Nature; a great book; a breathtaking view; an incredible movie; a enchanting set of eyes; chocolate with almonds; a gorgeous set of "Tina Turner legs"; a beautiful red Rose; a set of sweet luscious lips; a heart melting singing voice; sweet petite breast;…and the list goes on and on.

The "Beautiful side of LIFE," and the beautiful things in LIFE should be shared with the special people in one's LIFE. And when they are, it makes the "beautiful side of LIFE" even more beautiful.

        SIR FINIS DeMILO BREWER
           1/16/2014..10:03 pm

BOOK II

# LOVE
## ...My Favorite
## SUBJECT

The naked Truth about a few,

that taught me ...

...about LOVE

March 5, 1:26a.m- Easter Sunday

While out with my friend today, I picked up 10 books today at the thrift store. I love it when I see a sign saying 5 books for .99 cents. I think everyone should buy at least 5 books a month; or even a week. Going into a Thrift Store and seeing a sign saying, "Books priced individually" is a travesty. Knowing they received them all for free, and they want to get a thrift store assigned retail price...madness.

One of the books I picked up I know is going to be one of my favorites. When it comes to the subject of LOVE, I'm the sucker at the top of the list. It's written by a LOIS SMITH BRADY, and she is a New York Times Columnist living in Bridgehampton. I wouldn't have a clue of where that is. I'm sure it is minus many with my innate complexion. but that's just how things tend to still pan out even after so many chances for us to learn to be more loving and diverse as Souls. And less hating, and economically & culturally group as humans. We all will to be returning to the FATHER (GOD) from whence we all come one day; and the last I heard, it's not segregated by color or culture.

Now back to the subject of LOVE...In spite of my two divorces, I did love my children's mother; I believe that is a requirement mandated by GOD when it comes to the children.

"...Husbands, love your wives."

This means one wife at a time. I was married to each of my wives 7 years apart. It is not advocating polygamy, like some might interpret. (Mormons, sex addicts, crazies, selfish, and any other group that read this wrong). I also believe that it makes a difference when children are born to parents that LOVE each other. It sets the stage for them to have a healthy disposition, and a feeling of security. A child senses more than society has realized because remember, it was only recently that they left heaven.

In Life, and in marriage, LOVE must be mutual, like minded, and not defy the natural law of GOD...

*"...let them be male & female, and not close kin."*

And not taken for granted. I think at some point my Love for each wife was taken for granted, and they were fooled into believing that the "bird in the bush, was better than the bird in the hand." I learned this lesson very early in life that this is not true. When someone LOVES you already (not learning how to love you, or trying to learning your likes & dislikes), then you are already at an advantage. The LOVE that that person has for YOU...

*"ain't no mountain high enough, or valley low enough"*

To keep them from getting YOU, whatever your pure heart desire. Because GOD will help them and your pure loving heart, to have whatever YOU desire.

Now please...I beg of you; DON'T confuse your Lust driven Sex, for LOVE. LUST is not of or from GOD; it's of the devil with its satanic attributes, and is infused with the elements of Deception. So I won't be discussing this subject here at the moment. So those of you that are enthralled in a LUSt filled SeX driven satanically orchestrated relationship liaison…when I mention LOVE I'm not talking to YOU.

Well…I guess I'll get to reading my book. In the meantime, I'll share a few stories with you about some of my LOVE "lesson". Some are a bit shocking, and all of them were Life changing for me. I do harbor a few regrets because looking back now, I wish some would have been handled differently. I realize the younger I was, the less daring I was. Back then I had a problem with age, and even though I've been in love with some pretty young souls, I didn't believe a real young person could teach me anything about LOVE. But LIFE has constantly brought experiences to me, to un-train me of my way of thinking. And I fought it, time and time again. Until the one day when I was a much older Man, and I fell in LOVE with a much younger girl. And in that experience, I was set free and released from "LOVE bondage" and my discrimination toward the young "minds".

These words were spoken to me as clear as day; and with the natural Law of GOD concerning romantic LOVE recessed in my mind the voice said,

*"Pure LOVE, comes from a Pure Heart; and only a Young Heart*

*… can show Pure untainted LOVE."*


*From that day on, I no longer fought against the attraction that I so often found myself in. Looking into the "windows of the Soul", I would see something in their eyes, and they would notice something in mine, and then would begin the journey of LOVE at first sight for me, over & over yet again.*

## My KURSTENs

My very, very first Kursten I was in love with was when I was in the 6$^{th}$ grade; she was in the fifth. Back then at my little elementary school that gave us a very sheltered life (in McClendonville), students in different grades often would find themselves in the same classroom. I believe my Teacher was a Mrs. Rogers; she was the only white Teacher there at the time, and I loved her to death.

The school was called P.S. Lawton, clarified as Peter Simon Lawton, and was the only elementary school in the area of our neighbor. It has been torn down now for many years, and the area was made into a neighborhood park. The "clown" that made that decision to have the school tore down should have been fired the same day, and denied their pension. For it held great memories for all of us kids growing up in this part of New Orleans. Looking back now, it was like living in Mayberry; there were no bad kids in our school. Well except for one; he made the News. I don't remember all the details, but the school was held under siege for several hours as this sixth grader had a gun pointed at the school while he was hidden in an adjacent vacant lot. I remember being told by our teacher to stay low as we all we also were instructed to stayed away from the windows in the classroom…it was a very crazy day that day.

Spelled differently, anyone that was familiar with this neighborhood knew that it was not pronounced the same way the name was spelled. McClendonville was called Ma-clina-ville, and went from Tita

Street on the Westside of the neighborhood covering Oden St., Horace St., Flanders St., and Witz lane & Lee's Lane on the Eastside. It was a great time growing up for me, and Kursten was a great addition to my prepubescent Love Life in our little "Mayberry" part of New Orleans.

Kursten sat one row over from me in my class at Lawton. Her pretty black hair combed in a ponytails on each side, and one at the back, she was one of the prettiest girls there. There were no hair extensions, or wigs worn by girls back then. A girl's hair was either "pressed" or worn natural. And if ya mama & or daddy had "good hair", you were blessed to have "good hair" too. The other girls in the class were probably jealous of Kursten, and the boys were flocking to her like flies. Pulling her hair from time to time like little boys do, as a sign of saying, "I like you."

I never pulled Kursten's hair, and our little love affair may have lasted a month. Relationships weren't never long for a kid in elementary. Even as I got older, my average was three months; but I always had a girlfriend.

Like all my "Love affairs" of old, there was hardly ever anything more than us holding hands (which was a milestone), and if you got a chance to kiss, it was just a lil peck on the cheek. Now I don't know what everybody else was doing, but that's all I was doing at 8 & 9 years old.

By the time I went to junior high, I don't think I ever got to see Kursten again. As famous as the name Brady was for us growing up, she was a Brady I was in love with way before I ever knew Marsha, Jane, or Cindy.

When I reached the 8$^{th}$ grade, I had a brief encounter with another Kursten; a pretty little 7$^{th}$ grader from my neighborhood. She was from the Roschilds family, and they were known for having pretty daughters. We never became an item because there was another girl liking me also, that was a friend of Kursten. And when this girl from a different neighborhood (The Cut-off) found out I was liking Kursten and not her, she told Kursten,

"He just wants you for your stuff."

It's laughable now, but it wasn't then. And Kursten being the pretty little naïve 7$^{th}$ grader that she was, what could she do? She didn't know anything; she was not going to trust me...an older guy in the 8$^{th}$

grade? And it didn't matter that I was from her own neighborhood.

I knew she liked me the same as I her, and wanted to "go together" as we called it then. But peer pressure overruled it. I would see her occasionally throughout the years, and we remained neighborhood friends.

To this day, I'm very fond of her mother, and see her often in church. I give her a hug & kiss when I see her because she knew me when I was Youth Pastor when I first started out in the Ministry. She was a member at this same church, and she used to tell me how she enjoyed my message when I preached.

I learned years ago that Kursten passed many years earlier, and I was so shocked to hear this. I also heard about her sons that she had, and how they grew up with quite a neighborhood reputation for robbing, stealing & killing. They were called the 'Roschilds boys", and died at a young age also. I'm very fond of Kursten's mother Mrs. Roschilds; she's up in age now. Strangely though, she isn't even aware of how fond I was... of her $2^{nd}$ youngest daughter.

Now the first two Kursten is what initiated my involvement with the next Kursten. And this Kursten (Jackson) is what lead me to the final Kursten, Miss Sangi.

By the time I met the $3^{rd}$ Kursten, I was already in high school. And the most crazy part of all, she was still in elementary.

I believed we shared two summers together, and I think the first one was, when she was still in fifth grade.

Years ago, I would have never written this down, spoke it out loud within ear-shot of another human being, or admitted this to myself. And I definitely would have never written it down for someone else to read in a book of mine. But I have grown, I have matured, I have evolved. I can face my TRUTHS because they are mine, it is a part of my life, and they actually happened. And I think it is very healthy that we not only face them, but also understand why they are.

I thank GOD that I can face the TRUTHS in my life. At first I never understood why these things were happening all the time. But I have learned something about myself, and about Life. And because of my relationship with GOD, I was able to see both sides of the "coin".

This is how I've come to understand it. From the GOD-side, the LORD has given me the "gift of dealing with, and understanding young people. For this is an asset, when it comes to preaching to this group of unique individuals, and trying to reach them. But from the carnal-human side, satan knew it was a gift, and like all gifts from GOD, he will try to make your gift work against you. He wasn't going to just let me be, without causing trouble. So sometimes in my puberty stages of trying to understand my own body, and the hormones that were raging, some of these encounters had sexual overtones. But my being who I am, and growing up reading the Bible as a kid, I knew that I was not suppose to have sex while I was young, and not married. And at the age of 15-18, no one in this age group of mine was rushing to get married. There was sex going on, but no marriage. So for all of my girlfriends & "crushes" that was happening in my life, if you were a virgin when I met you, you were still one when we broke up. And as for the "crushes", I wrote about them and dreamed about them, but nothing was going on in the dark.

Now understand, from a natural human side, the desire for sex was always there. But from a spiritual side, I just didn't think it was right for me to take a girl's virginity and be responsible for her being "wild & loose" later on. Because we all know that once that door is open, it can no longer be closed.

Sexual experiences are by design, a very time-sensitive event that has already been factored into our lives by GOD. If you open that door too soon, you are going to have a teenage (or preteen) daughter problem. At a very young age, they will have sexual desires that will control them, without them having a clue as to why they can't control it. We all have heard of numerous stories of young girls 12 & 13 doing some very "grown-up" things; defying their moms. All just to please some boy or over 18 yrs old man. Trying to satisfy this new experience of making their body shake & shiver like crazy and feel things it has never felt before, without knowing why.

So during those times when I found girls wanting to "do it" as it was called then, I was struggling with the desire to Not. My putting them on a pedestal, and being seen by them as a "good guy", started very early in my life. Even though I was not angel, I just valued their virginity more than they valued it themselves. And I learned that no matter how "prim or proper" they were, or loud & ghetto, 95% of girls want to have sex without their parents knowing.

In my crazy life growing up, I never wanted a normally life; and I can't even explain why I felt this way. And because of this crazy prayer I prayed to GOD, and HIS law of the Universe where HE wrote in HIS Word (The Bible)...

*"...You have what You say";*

I have gotten just what I've asked for. My Life has been far from average, or normal.

Looking back, I realize that if it wasn't for some of these experiences, I would not be sitting here writing. You would not be sitting where you are reading this book, because this Book would not exist.

Having been deemed by Life to some degree, as a pretty experienced person (loosely claimed expert) in the area of the subject of LOVE, I believe I can help people in this particular area of Life. For many are very confuse when it comes to the subject, and many confuse the subject when it comes to SEX.

Now of all the beautiful young "Pure Hearts" that I have LOVED, there have never been a sexual relationship. I can admit from experience that the desire to do more was there (that's natural), but wisdom (according to the Bible) taught me early that...

> "there was a Time and Place for everything, under the Sun".

Desiring a sexual experience with someone you love is as natural as the desire to eat. But like all desires in life, there is a Time associated with it. Nature (GOD) has established that Time, and if we as intelligent beings would take heed, and pay attention to HIS time-clock, the self-induced problems that we have created in society, would not exist.

The emphasis on going to college is more important in today's society than the concept of marriage. Yet the girls/young women are still having babies, still having sex, and sexual diseases are still very rampant.

By the time most girls reach the age of 15 yrs old, the sexual drive that was diminished as a child, would have awaken by its natural time-clock. This is why so many get pregnant around this age.

Because of the natural course of Life would have already prepared the body for Motherhood. The menstrual would have started, the young women would be getting married and preparing to raise a family. But in today's society, getting married at 15 or 18 yrs old is considered crazy. And even 19-25 yrs old is discouraged. Yet most in this age group are having sex, multiple partners, and having babies. Some are even "jumping the fence" and joining the "same sex" movement, in what I call the "greedy/nasty" sex. They so nasty & greedy they want to go both ways.

If the generations of old, and today would read the Bible...

"and not lean to their own understanding",

they would get a sense of why GOD has set the plan in place that he has. But look around; we have created this mess. Teenage pregnancy is not the problem it used to be a few years ago. The biggest problem you may have with your 15 yr old today is kissing & having sex with another 15 yr old girl. Sometime they are as young as 12 yrs old. Because this world has gotten itself,

> "screw-up, twisted, and perverted"

...in the head, the heart, and between the legs. And it's the same for the young boys; they are just as confuse as the young girls. And dumb permissive adults/parents are just sitting around "dumb" like it is normal for a boy to like a boy, and a girl to kiss a girl.

Growing up, I spent a few Summers at my Aunt Marla house. She is really my cousin

Marla that grew up with our mom, but we love her so that we call her Aunt.

Kursten's mom lived next door to my Aunt Marla; they both were good friends. Kursten was friends with my cousin Celes (Aunt Marla's daughter), and they hung out like girls do.

Kursten's mom also had a lil sister that was closer to my age, and she saw me the times she would visit next door. I would be babysitting for my Aunt Marla occasionally, so I found myself in the company of Kursten & my cousin often. For some reason Kursten's aunt started teasing her about liking me, and at the time we were only just friends. So after being teased often enough, I guess some how the idea didn't seem so ridiculous to us after all. So we stuck around and saw each other whenever I was over at my

Aunt. We didn't do anything other than talk and enjoy the fun of being boyfriend & girlfriend. My mother having as many boys as she did, some of us were known for cleaning up real good, and for some reason I can remember being summons from my Aunt's by Kursten's mom next door to help Kursten and her brother Curt to clean-up their house. Again let me remind you... my Aunt Marla & Kursten's mom were very good friends.

Kursten and I spent most of our opportunities together during the Summer. If I saw her doing the school year, it was on the weekend...a time spent helping them clean-up. And there is one weekend that I have never forgotten. It was the first time we kissed. And it was the one kiss I remember the most... ...it was magical!

I was leaving their house after spending a few hours of helping her & her brothers clean. She walked me to the door, and even though it was to make sure the door was locked, we both had a few other ideas in mind too. At the door, we stole a few moments alone. Then I kissed her. It was a long passionate kiss. It lasted for only 3 or 4 seconds, but it seems like a lifetime. And just like in the old movies where they show a man & a woman kissing and fireworks or bursting like the Fourth of July, I saw the same image. I literally saw stars, and I can't even explain it. There were actual stars I saw with my eyes closed, so I knew they had to get the idea from somewhere.

I have never experienced that with anyone since. So you know I was hooked. For her age she was well developed; and for her kiss, that had to be a certified confirmation that there was something incredibly awesome, extraordinary, and very unusual happening between us. We must have been Soul-mates in another life, because there was no other way for me to explain it...She was only eleven; I was 15 going on sixteen, and the girl literally "rocked my world!"

In our two summers we shared, that's the most we ever done...Kiss. And because of this, she has always meant the world to me, and always will.

I remember the summer we broke up. My cousin Celes called me early one Saturday morning to come over. She said Kursten wanted me. So I think by 10a.m., I was sitting on my Aunt's sofa and Kursten was there with me. She had on some pretty white shorts, and I could tell she had something heavy on her mind. My aunt was at work, Kursten's mom was at work, and we had the house all to ourselves.

What she wanted was to break-up; she was going to the 7$^{th}$ grade after the Summer was over, and I could see that she was excited about her being around boys her age. Well I knew instinctively that it was a bad idea, because she was much more mature than the little boys that she was getting excited about. They were still wanting to play games; hide-& seek, cops & robbers, dodge-ball. And she was turning 12 yrs old, and wanting someone to love her, tell her how pretty & beautiful she was, hold hands, spend time together, and share an occasional kiss.

Well after only a few months of putting up with the little boys and their games they were still playing, she was calling me to get back together. I remember the day, and I refused; and it was so foolish of me. I have always regretted my harshness to turning her down, even if it was in a very nice way. I loved her more than I loved any girlfriend of mine at that point in my life; would have spent the rest of my life with her. But I was too immature to understand that we are allowed to make mistakes, and allowed to change our minds when we realize we have.

I don't know it Kursten ever finished school, but I learned she got with some older guy and she got hooked on drugs real bad. And even to this day, she has never been herself again; the self I knew and loved.

I've met her only daughter for the first time last Thanksgiving. The family was invited to the Thanksgiving dinner my brother hosted for our family. Kursten's two brothers Curt & Calvin was there along with their wives and kids; but Kursten did not come. I was looking forward to seeing her. It had probably been more than 15 years since I'd seen her, and more than 35 years since she was the reason I smiled in the Summer time.

Sometimes a young girl doesn't know her value or worth, and she stumbles into the wrong arms trying to find it. All my life GOD has given me the ability to see the worth of every female I've ever met in my life. Even those I've only seen from a distance (strangers, celebrities, "ships passing"). The value of every women, young girl, female child has been proclaimed, mandated, and deemed irrefutable by GOD. It is not determined or based on the affection or the amount of attention you get from a male person (or female person). When one has a personal relationship with GOD, Creator of all things, you know where you fit in, and you KNOW your Worth. It's not externally derived...but an inborn gift and attribute that comes with you when you leave from Heaven and come down here to earth as a Baby. But if you are born in a society or environment where the true essence of GOD is not there, and instead you are born in an atmosphere of Lies, false religions, foolish cultural practices, and dumb family traditions, the TRUTH of who you are is hidden from you. And it causes problems for you...and the society as a whole. The practice of discarding female babies in the Asian & India cultures, and favoring males is a prime example of this stupidity.

## Miss Sangi / Na-She

Only Nine years old when I met her; I was already Seventeen years old, graduated from high school, and was attending college. I don't how it happen, but it did. Whether I can call it an accident or not, is yet to be determined. But I do know that just like accidents, this was one incident that was not planned, and forever changed my Life.

Now I don't know if Miss Sangi remembers any of this because in spite of maturity, and intelligence, she was very young. The only thing that I can remember about being 9 yrs old is I remember telling myself that it was the best year of my Life...ever. I don't know why, I don't know if something happens to me, or if something in us changes spiritually at 9, but I remember really enjoying myself at this age.

After graduating High school in May 1979, I was on a plane to California the next day. It was my first time leaving home, and I was very excited,

I was going to be staying in Pasadena by Beverly. She had a daughter with my oldest brother when he was 18, and she was 36 from what I heard. This was my brother's first child, my mother's first Grand-child, and my favorite niece at the time, because she was born on my birthday. I spent a few weekends babysitting for Beverly growing up, so I was like a member of the family. But before Miss Sangi, there was Na-She.

Twelve years old, very smart, and thin as they come. But I sure was in love with everything about her. I believe I had already made Eighteen, because I remember us being 6 years apart.

Every night we shared the same room; I slept in the bottom bunk, and she slept in the top. Every day she practiced her violin, and every day I had a front row seat to the command performance. She was still learning, but it was music, and pure joy to me to listen to her.

I used to call her Saturn Eyes because of the soft light dark rings that noticeably encircled her eyes. I think there is a medical name for the condition, but I didn't see it as a medical condition. I felt it added to her unique qualities, and perfect beauty.

I spent two summers with Na-She, and even was with the family one time during the fall; loved every moment of it, but we never acknowledge what we felt for each other. But when you have those kinds of feelings for someone, you know without saying a word.

During the Fall when I stayed with them, every morning after her two brothers Mike & Leo had caught the bus to school, I would walk my niece to school. Beverly would have already left for work. By the time I had made it back, Na-she would be just getting out of the tub, and getting ready to get dress for school. This happen every morning for 9 months; And due to the trust that I know Beverly had in me as a young man, I must have been in some kind of trance, because any thoughts of doing anything behind her back seemed to be blocked. We both knew that we were "liking" each other; we slept in the same room every night, she in the top bunk, and I in the bottom; and we were home alone every morning for at least an hour. But we both behaved ourselves.

Now one morning, something different occurred. And it has puzzled me every since. I can't say for certain what was going through her head, but it was like I was under some kind of trust spell. Because it was two or three days later before it dawn on me what took place. Now all my life I have been known for being the "good boy", but this is one time I would have retired the position for a few hours. And only would have been good to the love of my life in the room.

This particular morning, I had made it back from walking my "birthday buddy" to school, and Na-She was still in the tub. I sat down to watch TV, and I know nothing that interesting was on it, but somehow I was in a trance. A few minutes later,

Na-She came out of the bathroom with just a towel on; she had never done this before. She stood just a few feet away from me asking me a question. To this day I couldn't tell you what the question was, what I answered, or what was on the TV. But it was either the next day or several days later that I realized what had happen. Who comes out of a bathroom from taking a bath, wrapped in nothing but a towel, to ask the person they "like" a question without having something else in mind? Who does that?...No one!

I beat myself up for many years after this for ignoring what I realized was a "hint" to a great Romeo & Juliet experience.

 Now I could be wrong because I have never got her side of the story, but I know one thing; let the record show. We both would have saw "stars" that morning, she would have never made it to school, and I would have spent the rest of my life making her the happiest girl in the world. Beverly would have had to forgive me, but I can't speak for the War part, but...

"...*All is fair in Love*"

After that year, I returned home to New Orleans; I didn't get to see Na-She again for many years. When I saw her again, she was married and so was I. I was living back in New Orleans after living in Arizona for more than 10 years.

Beverly had also moved to New Orleans at that point, and she was graduating late in life with a degree in Engineering; I was at the graduation because someone else I knew had invited me. And while there, I happen to see Beverly. And to my surprise, Na-She also; she was there with her husband and kids. When we both saw each other, I remember us both nearly knocked over chairs getting to one another. Hugs & Hi's were in order, and if our spouses weren't a few feet away, a stolen long overdue kiss may have been the biggest heist of the day.

As I was writing this, I thought that maybe I should conceal the identities a bit so that no discord is produced by current lovers. But I decided against it. For years I've never liked when a Writer would hide the identity of the people in their stories to "protect the innocent". I said the day I "pen" my books, I wasn't changing names. But then a friend called me and we had a discussion about the subject. After the conversation, I decided to "change the names" to protect the innocent, the guilty, and the bystanders.

Let me add though, we all have a past, and "No Man" is an Island. All our lives are connected to other lives, so we best come to terms with the things that happened in our past life. If we don't, it might be a bit shocking for us on the day when we hear pieces of our lives being told by someone who was also there, and directly involved. Some may think it's an invasion of privacy, but it's not. They are telling their version; which we all have a right to do. If you find that they have embellished their version a bit, then you have the option to tell your version. Because we all know that there is more than one side to every TRUE STORY.

## Back To Miss Sangi

The Autumn of my first year of college, I lived on the dorm the first semester. But by the 2$^{nd}$ Semester, I was back home at my mom's house. Dorm life was nothing but drugs, partying, and ex-virgins morphing into sluts; and I didn't want any part of it. I felt females should have shown a lot more respect for themselves. Some spend their whole lives "saving it," and then get to college and give it away like it was candy. They were away from home now, and whatever they had been holding on to while they were at home, was now a "free for all". And the line was forming out the door of the dorms.

And here in 2015, it's a whole lot worse here in this Social media era where "anything goes", and bisexual and trisexual is the latest excuse being used for being "nasty & trifling". And the young men today are just as nasty. Some of them on the "down-low" lying to themselves, their girlfriends, and their parents.

So my $2^{nd}$ semester of college began my four summer experience of Love Lessons from Nine year old Miss Sangi.

My three best friends have always been females. And they are my three friends even today, after almost 40 years.

Each of these friends all had cousins, and in each instance, I was also friends with these cousins. Now these were innocent times; a lot of girls just didn't take off their clothes at the drop of a hat. And those that did, I steered far away from them anyway. I didn't want no" baby mamas" in my life, and I definitely didn't want history repeating itself, if I slipped and accidently had one.

So in the Autumn of 1980, I was going home every weekend from college because I chose not to deal with the endless traffic of "loose girls" and the doggish mentality of my adjoining roommates.

My time was spent many weekends and nights at my best friend Darla's house. We would play games, and watch TV till the wee hours of the morning. Barney Miller was my late night favorite, "Mash" was Darla's favorite, and if nothing was on, we just played games till we got tired. Of course this was before cable when you still wrestled with the antenna to get a good picture.

Darla was already a teenage mother, and the baby Daddy was my friend. Sometimes Darla would slip over to my uncle's house and hang-out with him. I would be left with the two cousins and the friend that came over for the weekend. By Sunrise, I was heading back home to my house across the street, Darla had made it back to her house, and another weekend was over.

Now why her mother was very relaxed with me staying over I don't know, but it seem like I always got along with mothers. I don't know if it was my face, or something they saw in my eyes, but I was always allowed to spend a bit of time with an unusual number of young females growing up.

I remember the first night Miss Sangi and I was up all night. Darla was gone by my uncle, the rest had fallen asleep on the living room floor, and my lil friend Miss Sangi had bet me that she could stay awake with me all night. And amazingly, she did. And every weekend from then on, she came over to her friend's house. And every Summer, she spent the whole Summer. Together, we all had many great days & nights of laughing and playing. The Summer I spent in Pasadena (by Na-She), she never even came over I found out from Darla; not even once.

When school started again, and she found out that I was back in town, she was over the following weekend. We laughed about it then, but Miss Sangi and I both knew why she was missing in action that Summer.

This unspoken Romance, and impossible relationship we had, went on for 4 years straight. And for four years minus the time I was in Pasadena, I thought about Miss Sangi every single day. By the time she was Eleven, she was almost 6' feet tall, full developed, and fine as a glass of wine. But her mind was pure as the driven snow...so I thought.

Wrestling for two years with whether she was feeling the same about me as I was about her, and ignoring the obvious chemistry that was undeniable, one day I found out just how much she loved me. And I was shocked; I didn't think young people could think like that. But that was the beginning of the end of our mutual relationship from that day on.

She had a diary like all girls have at that age, and one weekend she brought it over. I don't remember how it fell in my lap, but I think it was intentional. Well, in this diary, she had written how she went to bed every night thinking about me making love to her. I was stunned, mouth wide open surprised. I was like,

"little 12 year old girls don't talk, write, or even think like this...no way!"

But a big part of me was also relieved; she loved me just like I loved her. And it was so very exciting to know, because now I didn't have to guess, wonder, and wreck my brain trying to figure out if I was imagining it all. But this also created a problem.

She was fine!...but only twelve. No one alive would even think she was just a kid. Nature had been sooo very good to her, and it was sooo very unfair to me. In spite of what she wanted, and in spite of what I wanted, I know we could not have Sex; she was a mere child even though her body (thanks to nature) was sending very mixes signals. Plus I wasn't that brave & daring back then. I was frustrated; very frustrated; and this is where the mistake was made.

Miss Sangi favorite friend that she was close with; the one she came over and hung out with, liked me too. She was 19 yrs old, but I didn't like her like that. We were all friends. We all got along, and they all knew Miss Sangi and I was an item; even if it was not openly said. The body language between us was obvious, the conversations we had were "A & B", and the blushing we did when we saw each other on Friday night was ridiculous. And after many months of dealing with not being able to be with each other physically because the love of my life was not old enough, in spite of how well built she was, I said the hell with it, and slept with the older friend. This was the biggest regret of my life back then.

When she found out, it was World War I, II, & III all roll up into one in that little young mind, and pure heart. T

he screaming and yelling she did was pretty incredible; and I was very shocked. I had never seen that kind of anger in a person that young in my life. It was no different than a husband betraying a wife, because the hurt she felt cut to her very Soul. And from that day on, I respected a person's age, but no longer judge them by it.

Love is Love; and Pain is Pain, and it all feels the same no matter your age. Reactions may vary, and the words expressed may differ, but it all feels the same no matter our age, our culture, our color, our economic background.

She didn't speak to me for a long time, and I spent the next two years trying to make it up to her. A year later, she got pregnant by one of the nappy head boys in her school. I know it was not planned, and I know I was mad as hell. I couldn't do anything about it though. What goes around always comes back around; I devastated her, and she devastated me. But in both cases both incidents, were never intentional.

She miscarried the child several months later, and it was close enough to term that a burial had to be arranged. For the child. Of course there was no way that I would attend the funeral; it would look suspicious.

The night she was in the hospital alone after having the miscarriage I really wanted to go and sit with her. But I wondered about the strange looks I would get from the Nursing staff; they knew she was a child, and they would easily see that I was not. Plus, I didn't think I wanted to be accused of fathering the child, when I know my eyes hadn't even seen the "cookie" let alone knew what it taste like. If I'm going to catch hell, at least let me be guilty of the crime.

Miss Sangi went on with her life; graduating, marrying and doing well. For many years afterwards I would see her, and still had butterflies. But I learned to live with them; then one day I realized the butterflies were no longer there. Just genuine CARE for an ol' friend.

Of course, after four years of being in love with someone, I could share a lot more of the events that occurred between us; but I rather the memories of the rest of them to remain in the recesses of my mind. It's in the past now; I'd like it to remain there.

In all these Love Lessons, not once was there ever an attempt at having Sex. I learned early that Sex is like a door. And once you open it, you cannot close it back. And if a person is very young when they are exposed to this "force" it will be a driving force in almost everything they do for the next few years, until the desire subsides. And it will.

So I never wanted to be responsible for opening those "doors" with any young person.

Now being a hormonal teenager and an avid reader growing up, I read Johnson &

Johnson Sex book, and was participant in some experiments to confirm some of the theories they expressed. But that's all these incidents were for me, just experimentations.

I've been accused & called gay and fag over the years. Even been told I must like "only young pussy" by an older female that I was not being cooperative to her discreet advances. And I was even called, and looked at strange because I didn't get excited by girls on stripper poles, porn, or G-strings in the crack of their Ass.

 I'm a simple guy, with simple taste. And if I was gay, I'd be a lesbian cause I only like women. And if it was only "young pussy" that I liked, I would have "F" everything I had a chance to "F" growing up. Once when I was 17, I found myself lying in the same bed with five young females under

16; we were chilling watching movies. If I was a dog, there would have been a whole lot of de-flowering going on that night. But I had too much respect for the opposite sex then, and still do now. And getting married would have been dumb if it was all about getting "young stuff" when there is so much young stuff being given away ever second of the day.

But I didn't cast my "pearls to the swine" then, and I don't now. I like the good things in life, and a stinky used up whore who loves being oogled by lots of strange men is not my idea of a good thang...no matter how young they are. I've also been accused of being arrogant, but I'm not. I just know what I like, and definitely know what I DON'T like.

In 1999 after my first divorce, I had pretty much felt that my placing females on a pedestal, was a waste of time. It seem like they all wanted to be "F" like a female dog, and treated like one as well. But I was not going to be the treator to the treatee. I'm a Gentleman by nature & design, and I'm not going to change my "stripes" for "spots" to suit no one.

## The FINAL CHAPTER

Here in 2015, who would have thought in my lifetime I would see the things that I see going on today from a moral stand point. Anything & everything goes...kissing a girl is a popular song and pass-time for pre-teens, boys are holding hands in school, parents are clueless to their kids adult activities, and society is passing Laws saying it's all ok. And when the judgment of GOD falls on this generation, there won't be a dry eye in Hades.

Recently while watching "Girls Rock" I was amazed at the message that's being preached to young girls today. The roles in life has become twisted, mixed-up, and blurred. A continual message of "I don't need a man" is being forced fed to this generation of young girls. While satan is sneaking in telling them go ahead "kiss a girl".

Many societies before ours have thought they've had the answers to LIFE. They have tried many ideas, philosophies, and ways of living; and lots of them have strayed from the basic principles and instructions for living…the WORD of GOD.

I will not stray from these principals, I will not alter these principals, and I will not argue with the one who set them in place.

No matter who we are, or where we THINK we are going in this life, when we all get to the end of our roads, we will be judged on how well we did on the TEST called Life. And no matter who's opinion, philosophy, or lifestyle that you choose to embrace or promote, you will be judged by ONE…and only One. And it doesn't matter whether you believe in HIM, (and there is no damn "Her" no matter what the feminist say) or not, your fate will be determined by whether you agreed with the basic principles that HE has laid for all of mankind.

Many talk about the future, and all the plans that they have for this future that lies ahead. But there are "signs in the Heaven" that says, THIS "lost" GENERATION is in for a rude awakening. They don't know GOD, don't want to know HIM because their lifestyles don't agree with HIS rules; they don't follow HIS instructions, and they have "hewn out their own cisterns". And no matter how much of a future this "lost" generation "prophesize" to the Youths of today, there is no future unless GOD says so. And the last time I read what HE said, it doesn't look good. The "signs in the Heavens" (Four Blood Moons), the Harbingers, the earthquakes in divers places, and all the TRUE Prophets all agree…

…JESUS IS ON HIS WAY. And this generation will see…it 4 themselves.

If your plans, and your Life, don't agree with HIS plans HE outlined and suggested for your life (for GOD forces no one to do nothing), you will have your share of disappointments before you leave here.

And to me, one of the greatest disappointments you can have in

Life, is to believe something with all the passion possible, and live (or died) and find out it was not TRUE...all a LIE.

Of all the absolute TRUTHS I've learned in LIFE, one truth I've learned is...GOD is REAL.

And a few others I've learned is:

1. HE called me to preach HIS Gospel
2. JESUS is coming back
3. This Generation will see the $2^{nd}$ Coming of CHRIST
4. And there is no such thing as Gay

(the Beginning of)
# THE END

"Finis"...means the End in French

www.ingramcontent.com/pod-product-compliance
Lightning Source LLC
Chambersburg PA
CBHW071708040426
42446CB00011B/1974